The Damnable Life and Death of Stubbe Peeter

New York

Published by Curious Publications
697 Third Ave. #358
New York, NY 10017
curiouspublications.com

Copyright © 2025

ISBN-13: 979-8-9914395-6-5

This book faithfully reproduces the original 1590 pamphlet by George Bores. The text and images are in the public domain.

Cover design: Lela Hartzman

Printed and bound in the United States of America.

A NOTE ON THE TEXT

In 1589, a grim spectacle unfolded in the German town of Bedburg. A man named Peter Stump (also spelled Stumpf, Stubbe, or Stubbe) was accused of being a werewolf—and not just any werewolf, but one of the most monstrous in recorded lore.

His life, his gruesome crimes, and his thorough execution are detailed in this pamphlet from 1590, *The Damnable Life and Death of Stubbe Peeter*, written by George Bores.

Tortured into confession, Stump claimed he had practiced black magic since age twelve and pledged himself to the Devil.

"The Devil, who hath a ready ear to listen to the lewd motions of cursed men, promised to give him whatsoever his heart desired during his mortal life," the pamphlet stated. "Whereupon this vile wretch neither desired riches nor promotion, nor was his fancy satisfied with any external or outward pleasure, but having a tyrannous heart and a most cruel bloody mind, requested that at his pleasure he might work his malice on men, women, and children, in the shape of some beast, whereby he might live without dread or danger of life, and unknown to be the executor of any bloody enterprise which he meant to commit."

The Devil obliged, bestowing upon him a magical girdle, allowing him to transform into a ravenous wolf—"strong and mighty, with eyes great and large, which in the night sparkled like unto brands of fire, a mouth great and wide, with most sharp and cruel teeth, a huge body and mighty paws." Under this supposed spell, he admitted to a 25-year reign of terror.

According to his confession, Stump murdered and cannibalized fourteen children and two pregnant women, devouring their unborn fetuses. He confessed to killing his own son and feasting on the boy's brain "as a most savory and dainty delicious mean to staunch his greedy appetite." The allegations didn't stop there—Stump was also charged with incest, said to have fathered a child with his daughter and engaged in relations with a succubus sent by the Devil himself. It was a confession soaked in blood, sin, and supernatural horror.

His execution on October 31, 1589—before the date was celebrated at Halloween—was equally theatrical and brutal: he was strapped to a wheel, had his flesh torn with red-hot pincers, his limbs broken, and was finally beheaded before being burned. His daughter and mistress were also put to death for allegedly aiding in his crimes.

The story is one of many featured in Montague Summers' 1933 book, *The Werewolf*. While Summers, who also wrote extensively on witches and vampires, appeared to be a believer, modern scholars certainly debate the truth behind the werewolf of Bedburg (and any werewolves). Some view it as a politically or religiously motivated show trial during a time of intense Catholic-Protestant conflict. Others interpret it as an early example of how societies demonize outsiders or explain horrific crimes through the lens of folklore. Whether madman, scapegoat, or monster, Peter Stump remains one of history's most infamous werewolves.

This reproduction features the original pages of the booklet, along with a modern text treatment for easier reading. Both are equally disturbing.

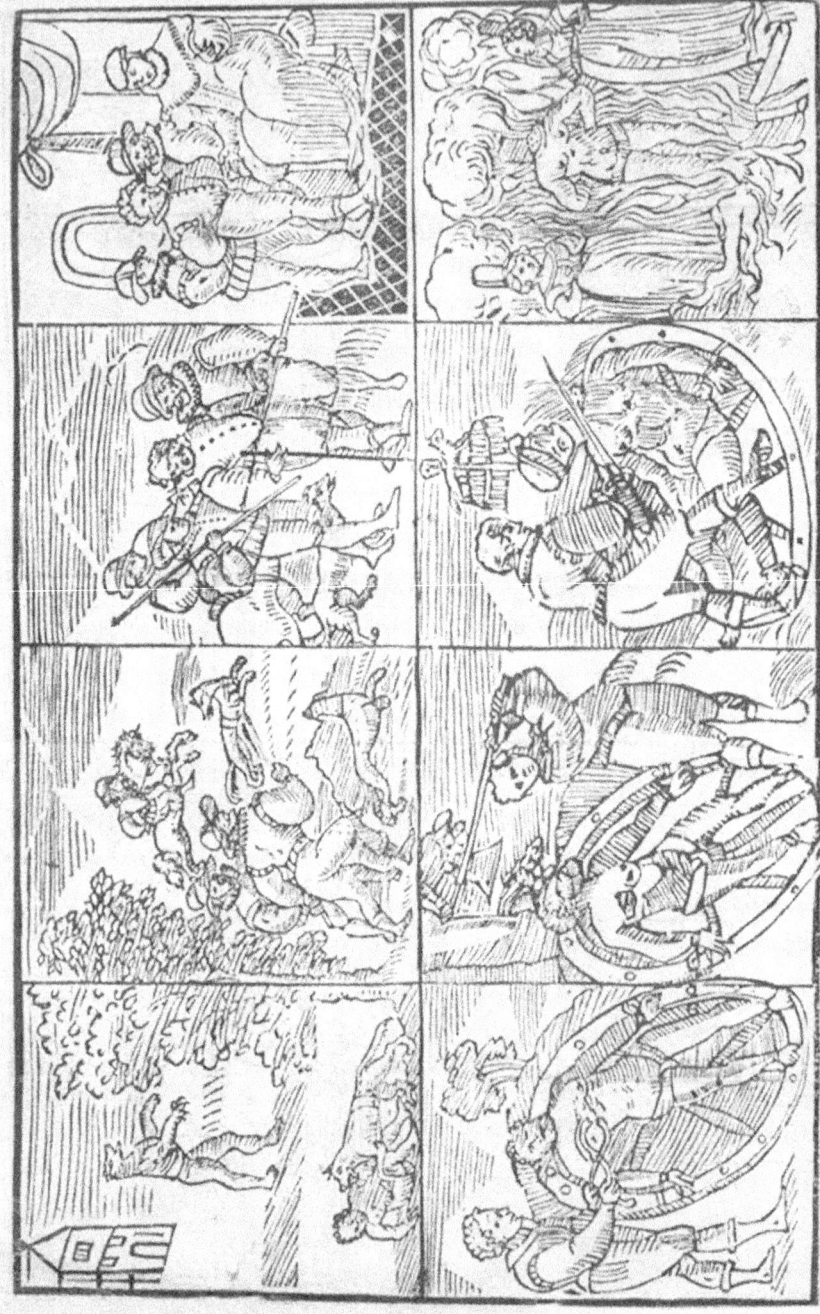

A true Discourse.
Declaring the damnable life and death of one Stubbe Peeter, a most wicked Sorcerer, who in the likenes of a Woolfe, committed many murders, continuing this diuelish practise 25. yeeres, killing and deuouring Men, Woomen, and Children.
Who for the same fact was taken and executed the 31. of October *last past in the Towne of* Bedbur neer the Cittie of *Collin* in *Germany.*

Trulye translated out of the high Duch, according to the Copie printed in Collin, brought ouer into England by George Bores ordinary Poste, the xj. daye of this present Moneth of Iune 1590. who did both see and heare the same.

AT LONDON
Printed for Edward Venge, and are to be *solde in* Fleet-street *at the signe of the* Vine.

¶ A most true Discourse,
declaring the life and death of one Stubbe Peeter, being a most wicked Sorcerer.

Those whome the Lord doth leaue to followe the Imagination of their own hartes, dispising his proffered grace, in the end through the hardnes of hart and contempt of his fatherly mercy, they enter the right path to perdicion and destruction of body and soule for euer: as in this present historie in perfect sorte may be seene, the strangenes whereof, together with the cruelties committed, and the long time therin continued, may driue many in doubt whether the same be truth or no, and the ratherfore that sundry false & fabulous matters haue hæretofore passed in print, which hath wrought much incredulitie in ye harts of all men generally, insomuch that now a daies fewe thinges do escape be it neuer so certain, but that it is embased by the tearm of a lye or false reporte. In the reading of this story, therfore I do first request reformation of opinion, next patience to peruse it, because it is published for examples sake, and lastly to censure thereof as reason and wisdome doth think conuenient, considering the subtilty that Sathan vseth to work the soules destruction, and the great matters which the accursed practise of Sorcery doth effect, the fruites whereof is death and destruction for euer, and yet in all ages practised by the reprobate and wicked of the earth, some in one sort, and some in another euen as the Deuill giueth promise to performe. But of all other that euer liued, none was comparable vnto this helhound, whose tiranny and cruelty did well declare he was of his Father the deuill, who was a murderer from the beginning, whose life and death and most bloody practises the discourse following doth make iust reporte.

In

In the townes of Cperadt and Bedbur neer vnto Collin in high Germany, there was continually brought vp and nourished one Stubbe Peeter, who from his youth was greatly inclined to euill, and the practising of wicked Artes euen from twelue yæers of age till twentye, and so forwardes till his dying daye, insomuch that surfeiting in the Damnable desire of magick, negromancye, and sorcery, acquainting him selfe with many infernall spirites and fæendes, insomuch that forgetting ye God that made him, and that Sauiour that shed his blood for mans redemption: In the end, careles of saluation gaue both soule and body to the deuil for euer, for small carnall pleasure in this life, that he might be famous and spoken of on earth, though he lost heauen thereby. The Deuill who hath a readye eare to listen to the lewde motions of cursed men, promised to giue vnto him whatsoeuer his hart desired during his mortall life: wherupon this vilde wretch neither desired riches nor promotion, nor was his fancy satisfied with any externall or outward pleasure, but hauing a tirannous hart, and a most cruell bloody bloudy minde, he only requested that at his plesure he might worke his mallice on men, Women, and children, in the shape of some beast, wherby he might liue without dread or danger of life, and vnknowen to be the executor of any bloudy enterprise, which he meant to commit: The Deuill who sawe him a fit instruemēt to persourm mischæfe as a wicked fænd pleased with the desire of wrong and destruction, gaue vnto him a girdle which being put about him, he was straight transsourmed into the likenes of a grædy deuouring Woolf, strong and mighty, with eyes great and large, which in the night sparkeled like vnto brandes of fire, a mouth great and wide, with most sharpe and cruell tæth, A huge body, and mightye pawes: And no sooner should he put off the same girdle, but presently he should appære in his former shape, according to the proportion of a man, as if he had neuer beene changed.

Stubbe Peeter hærwith was excædingly well pleased, and the shape fitted his fancye and agræed best with his nature, being inclined to blood and crueltye, therfore satisfied ed with this strange and diuelish gifte, for that it was not troublesome nor great in cariage, but that it might be hidden in a small room, he proceeded to the execution of sundry most hainous and vilde murders, for if any person displeased him, he would incontinent thirst for reuenge, and no sooner should they or any of theirs walke abroad in the fældes or about the Cittie, but in the shape of a Woolfe he would presentlye incounter them, and neuer rest till he had pluckt out their throates and teare their toyntes a sunder: And after he had gotten a taste hærof, he toke such pleasure and delight in shedding of blood, that he would night and day walke the Fælds, and work extreame cruelties. And sundry times he would goe through the Stræts of Collin, Bedbur, and Cperadt, in comely habit, and very ciuilly as one well knowen to all the inhabitants therabout, & oftentimes was he saluted of those whose frændes and children he had buchered, though nothing suspected for the same. In these places, I say, he would walke vp & down, and if he could spye either Maide, Wife or childe, that his

eyes

eyes liked or his hart lusted after, he would waite their issuing out of ye Cittie or town, if he could by any meanes get them alone, he would in the fœldes rauishe them, and after in his Wolvish likenes cruelly murder them: yea often it came to passe that as he walked abroad in the fœldes, if he chaunste to spye a companye of maydens playing together, or else a milking of their kine, in his Wolvishe shape he would incontinent runne among them, and while the rest escaped by flight, he would be sure to laye holde of one, and after his filthy lust fulfilled, he would murder her presentlye, beside, if he had liked or knowne any of them, look who he had a minde vnto, her he would pursue, whether she were before or behinde, and take her from the rest, for such was his swiftnes offœt while he continued a woolf: that he would outrunne the swiftest greyhound in that Countrye: and so muche he had practised this wickednes, that ye whole Prouince was feared by the cruelty of this bloddy and deuouring Woolfe. Thus continuing his diuelishe and damnable dædes within the compas of fewe yeeres, he had
murdered

murdered thirteene yong Children, and
two godly yong women bigge with Child,
tearing the Children out of their wombes,
in most bloody and sauedge sorte, and after
eate their hartes panting hotte and rawe,
which he accounted dainty morsells & best
agreeing to his Appetite.

Moreouer he vsed many times to kill
Lambes and Kiddes and such like beastes,
feeding on the same most vsually raw and
bloody, as if he had béene a naturall Woolfe
indéed, so that all men mistrusted nothing
lesse then this his diuelish Sorcerie.

He had at that time liuing a faire yong
Damosell to his Daughter, after whom he
also lusted most vnnaturallye, and cruellye
committed most wicked incesse with her,
a most groce and vilde sinne, far surmounting
Adultrye or Fornication, though the
least of the thrée doth driue the soule into
hell fier, except hartye repentance, and the
great mercy of God. This Daughter of
his he begot when he was not altogither
so wickedlye giuen, who was called by the
name of Stubbe Beell, whose beautye and
good grace was such as deserued commen-

uations of all those that knewe her: And such was his inordinate lust and filthye desire toward her, that he begat a Childe by her, dayly vsing her as his Concubine, but as an insaciate and filthy beast, giuen ouer to worke euill, with greedines he also lay by his owne Sister, frequenting her company long time euen according as the wickednes of his hart lead him: Moreouer being on a time sent for to a Gossip of his there to make merry and good cheere, ere he thence departed he so wunne the woman by his faire and flattering speech, and so much preuailed, y[e] ere he departed the house: he lay by her, and euer after had her companye at his commaund, this woman had to name Katherine Trompin, a woman of tall and comely stature of exceeding good fauour and one that was well esteemed among her neighbours. But his lewde and inordinat lust being not satisfied with the company of many Concubines, nor his wicked fancye contented with the beauty of any woman, at length the deuill sent vnto him a wicked spirit in the similitude and likenes of a woman, so faire of face and comelye of personage,

nage, that she resembled rather some heavenly Hellin then any mortall creature, so farre her beauty exceeded the choisest sorte of women, and with her as with his harts delight, he kept company the space of seuen yeeres, though in the end she proued and was found indeed no other then a she Deuil, notwithstanding, this lewd sinne of lecherye did not any thing asswage his cruell and bloody minde, but continuing an insatiable bloodsucker, so great was the ioye he took therin, that he accouted no day spent in pleasure wherin he had not shed some blood not respecting so much who he did murder, as how to murder and destroy them, as the matter ensuing doth manifest, which may stand for a speciall note of a cruell and hard hart. For hauing a proper youth to his sonne, begotten in the flower and strength of his age, the firste fruite of his bodye, in whome he took such ioye, that he did commonly call him his Hartes ease, yet so farre his delight in murder exceeded the ioye he took in his only Sonne, that thirsting after his blood, on a time he inticed him into the feeldes, and from thence into a Forrest hard by, by, where making excuse to stay about the necessaries of nature, while the yong man went on forward, incontinent in the shape and likenes of a Wolfe he encountred his owne Sonne, and there most cruelly slewe him, which don, he presently eat the brains out of his head as a most sauerie and dainty delycious meane to staunch his grædye apetite: the most monstrous act that euer man heard off, for neuer was knowen a wretch from nature so far degenerate.

Long time he continued this wilde and villanous life, sometime in the likenes of a Wolfe, sometime in the habit of a man, sometime in the Townes and Citties, and sometimes in the Woods and thickettes to them adioyning, whereas the Duche coppye maketh mention, he on a time mette with two men and one woman, whom he greatly desired to murder, and the better to bring his diuelish purpose to effect, doubting by them to be ouermatched and knowing one of them by name, he vsed this pollicie to bring them to their end. In subtill sorte he conuayed himselfe far before them in their way and craftely couched out of their sight,

but

but as soone as they approched néere the place where he lay, he called one of them by his name, the partye hearing him selfe called once or twice by his name, supposing it was some familier fréend that in iesting sorte stood out of his sight, went from his companye towarde the place from whence the voice procéeded, of purpose to sée who it was, but he was no sooner entred within the danger of this transformed man, but incontinent he was murdered in y place, the rest of his company staying for him, expecting still his returne, but finding his stay ouer long: the other man lefte the woman, and went to looke him, by which means the second man was also murdered, the woman then séeing neither of both returne againe, in hart suspected that some euill had fallen vpon them, and therfore with all the power she had, she sought to saue her selfe by flight, though it nothing preuailed, for good soule she was also soone ouertaken by this light footed Wolfe, whom when he had first deflowred, he after most cruelly murdered, the men were after found mangled in the wood, but the womans body was neuer after

ter séene, for she the caitife had most rauenously deuoured, whose fleshe he estéemed both sweet and dainty in taste.

Thus this damnable Stubbe Peeter liued the tearme of fiue and twenty yéeres, vnsuspected to be Author of so many cruell and vnnaturall murders, in which time he had destroyed and spoyled an vnknowen number of Men, Women, and Children, Shéepe, Lambes, and Goates: and other Cattell, for when he could not through the warines of people drawe men, Women, or Children in his danger, then like a cruell and tirannous beast he would worke his cruelty on brut beasts in most sauadge sort, and did act more mischeefe and cruelty then would be credible, although high Germany hath béen forced to taste the trueth thereof.

By which meanes the inhabitantes of Collin, Bedbur and Cperadt, seeing themselues so gréeuously endaungered, plagued, and molested by this gréedy & cruel Woolfe, who wrought continuall harme and mischeefe, insomuch that few or none durst trauell to or from those places without good prouision of defence, and all for feare of this
devouring

deuouring and fierce woolf, for oftentimes the Inhabitants found the Armes & legges of dead Men, Women, and Children, scattered vp and down the fœlds to their great grœfe and vexation of hart, knowing the same to be done by that strange and cruell Woolfe, whome by no meanes they could take or ouercome, so that if any man or woman mist their Childe, they were out of hope euer to sœ it again aliue, mistrusting straight that the Woolfe had destroyed it.

And hære is to be noted a most strange thing which setteth forth the great power and mercifull prouidence of God to y comfort of eache Christian hart. There were not long agoe certain small Childzen playing in a Medowe together hard by y town, where also some store of kine were fœding, many of them hauing yong calues sucking vpon thē: and sodainly among these Childzen comes this vilde Woolfe running and caught a prittie fine Girle by the choller, with intent to pull out her throat, but such was y will of God, that he could not pearce the choller of the Childes coate, being high and very well stiffened & close claspt about her neck, and therwithall the sodaine great

B.   cry

crye of the rest of the childrē which escaped, so amazed the cattell feeding by, that being fearfull to be robbed of their young, they altogether came running against the Woolfe with such force, that he was presently compelled to let goe his holde and to run away to escape ye danger of their hornes, by which meanes the Childe was preserued from death, and God be thanked remains liuing at this day.

And that this thing is true, Maister Tice Artine a Brewer dwelling at Puddle-wharfe, in London, beeing a man of that Country borne, and one of good reputation and account, is able to iustifie, who is neere kiniman to this Childe, and hath from thence twice receiued Letters conserning the same, and for that the first Letter did rather driue him into wondering at the act then yælding credit therunto, he had shortlye after at request of his writing another letter sent him, wherby he was more fully satisfied, and diuers other persons of great credit in London hath in like sorte receiued letters from their freends to the like effect.

Likewise in the townes of Germany aforesaid continuall prayer was vsed vnto
god

god that it would please him to deliuer thē from the danger of this grædy Wolfe.

And although they had practised all the meanes that men could deuise to take this rauenous beast, yet vntill the Lord had determined his fall, they could not in any wise preuaile: notwithstanding they daylye continued their purpose, and daylye sought to intrap him, and for that intent continually maintained great mastyes and Dogges of muche strength to hunt & chase the beast wherſoeuer they could finde him. In the end it pleaſed God as they were in readines and prouided to méete with him, that they ſhould eſpye him in his woluiſhe likenes, at what time they beſet him round about, and moſte circumſpectlye ſet their Dogges vpon him, in ſuch ſort that there was no means to eſcape, at which aduantage they neuer could get him before, but as the Lord deliuered Goliah into ỹ handes of Dauid, ſo was this Wolfe brought in danger of theſe men, who ſéeing as I ſaide before no way to eſcape the imminent danger, being hardly purſued at the héeles preſently he ſlipt his girdle from about him, wherby the ſhape of a Wolfe cleane auoi-

B.ij. ded,

ded, and he appeared presently in his true shape & likenes, hauing in his hand a staffe as one walking toward the Cittie, but the hunters whose eyes was stedfastly bent vpon the beast, and seeing him in the same place metamorphosed contrary to their expectation: it wrought a wonderfull amazement in their mindes, and had it not bæne that they knewe the man so soone as they sawe him, they had surely taken the same to haue bæne some Deuill in a mans likenes, but for as much as they knewe him to be an auncient dweller in the Towne, they came vnto him, and talking with him they brought him by communication home to his owne house, and finding him to be the man indæde, and no selusion or phantasticall motion, they had him incontinent before the Matestrates to be examined.

Thus being apprehended, he was shortly after put to the racke in the Towne of Bedbur, but fearing the torture, he volluntarilye confessed his whole life, and made knowen the villanies which he had committed for the space of xxv. yæres, also he cōfessed how by Sorcery he procured of the Deuill a Girdle, which bæing put on, he forth forthwith became a Woolfe, which Girdle at his apprehension he confest he cast it off in a certain Vallye and there left it, which when the Maiestrates heard, they sent to the Vallye for it, but at their comming found nothing at al, for it may be supposed that it was gone to the Deuil from whence it came, so that it was not to be found. For the Deuil hauing brought the wretch to al the shame he could, left him to indure the torments which his dædes deserued.

After he had some space bæne imprisoned, the maiestrates found out through due examination of the matter, that his daughter Stubbe Beell and his Gossip Katherine Trompin, were both accessarye to diuers murders committed, who for the same as also for their leaud life otherwise committed, was arraigned, and with Stubbe Peeter condempned, and their seuerall Iudgementes pronounced the 28 of October 1589. in this manor, that is to saye: Stubbe Peeter as principall mallefactor, was iudged first to haue his body laide on a whæle, and with red hotte burning pincers in ten seueral places to haue the flesh puld off from the bones, after that, his legges and Armes to
be

be broken with a wooden Axe or Hatchet, afterward to haue his head strook from his body, then to haue his carkasse burnde to Ashes.

Also his Daughter and his Gossip were iudged to be burned quicke to Ashes, the same time and day with the carkasse of the aforesaid Stubbe Peeter. And on the 31. of the same moneth, they suffered death accordingly in the town of Bedbur in the presence of many pæres & princes of Germany.

Thus Gentle Reader haue I set down the true discourse of this wicked man Stub Peeter, which I desire to be a warning to all Sorcerers and Witches, which vnlawfully followe their owne diuelish imagination to the vtter ruine and destruction of their soules eternally, from which wicked and damnable practice, I beseech God keepe all good men, and from the crueltye of their wicked hartes. Amen.

After the execution, there was by the aduice of the Maiestrates of the town of Bedbur a high pole set vp and strongly framed, which first went through ye whæle whereon he was broken, whereunto also it

was

was fastened, after that a little aboue the Whœle the likenes of a Wœlfe was framed in wood, to shewe vnto all men the shape wherein he executed those cruelties. Ouer that on the top of the stake the sorcerers head it selfe was set vp, and round about the Whœle there hung as it were sixtéen péeces of wood about a yarde in length which represented the sixtœne persons that was perfectly knowen to be murdered by him. And the same ordained to stand therefor a continuall monument to all insuing ages, what murders by Stub Peeter was committed, with the order of his Iudgement, as this picture doth more plainelye expresse.

Witnesses that this is

true.

Tyse Artyne.
William *Brewar*.
Adolf Staedt.
George *Bores*.
With diuers others that haue seen the same.

A true Discourse.

Declaring the damnable life
and death of one Stubbe Peeter, a most wicked
Sorcerer, who in the likeness of a Wolf committed
many murders, continuing this devilish practice
25 Years, killing and devouring Men, Women, and
Children.

Who for the same fact was taken
and executed the 31st of October last past in
the town of Bedbur near the City of Collin
in *Germany*.

Truly translated out of the high Dutch, according to the copy printed in Collin, brought over into England by George Bores ordinary post, the 11th day of this present month of June 1590, who did both see and hear the same.

AT LONDON
Printed for Edward Venge, and are to be sold in
Fleet Street at the sign of the Vine.

A most true Discourse,
declaring the life and death of one Stubbe Peeter, being a most wicked sorcerer.

THOSE whom the Lord doth leave to follow the imagination of their own hearts, despising his proffered grace, in the end through the hardness of heart and contempt of his fatherly mercy, they enter the right path to perdition and destruction of body and soul for ever: as in this present history in perfect sort may be seen, the strangeness whereof, together with the cruelties committed, and the long time therein continued, may drive many in doubt whether the same be truth or no, and the rather fore that sundry false and fabulous matters have heretofore passed in print, which hath wrought much incredulity in the hearts of all men generally, insomuch that now of days few things do escape be it never so certain, but that it is embased by the term of a lie or false report.

In the reading of this story, therefore I do first request reformation of opinion, next patience to peruse it, because it is published for example's sake, and lastly to censure thereof as reason and wisdom doth think convenient, considering the subtlety that Satan useth to work the soul's destruction, and the great matters which the accursed practice of sorcery doth effect, the fruits whereof is death and destruction for ever, and yet in all ages practiced by the reprobate and wicked of the earth, some in one sort and some in another even as the Devil giveth promise to perform. But of all other that ever lived, none was comparable unto

OF STUBBE PEETER

this Hell hound, whose tyranny and cruelty did well declare he was of his father the devil, who was a murderer from the beginning, whose life and death and most bloody practices the discourse doth make just report.

In the towns of Cperadt and Bedbur near Collin in high Germany, there was continually brought up and nourished one Stubbe Peeter, who from his youth was greatly inclined to evil and the practicing of wicked arts even from twelve years of age till twenty, and so forwards till his dying day, insomuch that surfeiting in the damnable desire of magic, necromancy, and sorcery, acquainting himself with many infernal spirits and fiends, insomuch tat forgetting the God that made him, and that Savior that shed his blood man man's redemption: In the end, careless of salvation gave both soul and body to the Devil for ever, for small carnal pleasure in this life, that he might be famous and spoken of on earth, though he lost heaven thereby.

The Devil, who hath a ready ear to listen to the lewd motions of cursed men, promised to give him whatsoever his heart desired during his mortal life: whereupon this vile wretch neither desired riches nor promotion, nor was his fancy satisfied with any external or outward pleasure, but having a tyrannous heart and a most cruel bloody mind, requested that at his pleasure he might work his malice on men, women, and children, in the shape of some beast, whereby he might live without dread or danger of life, and unknown to be the executor of any bloody enterprise which he meant to commit.

The Devil, who saw him a fit instrument to perform mischief as a wicked fiend pleased with the desire of wrong and destruction, gave unto him a girdle which, being put around him, he was straight transformed into the likeness of a greedy, devouring wolf, strong and mighty, with eyes great and large, which in the night sparkled like unto brands of fire, a mouth great and wide, with most sharp and cruel teeth, a huge body and mighty paws. And no sooner should he put off the same girdle, but presently he should appear in his former shape, according to the proportion of a man, as if he had never been changed.

Stubbe Peeter herewith was exceedingly well pleased, and the shape fitted his fancy and agreed best with his nature, being inclined to blood and cruelty. Therefore, satisfied with this strange and devilish gift, for that it was not troublesome nor great in carriage, but that it might be hidden in a small room, he proceeded to the execution of sundry most heinous and vile murders; for if any person displeased him, he would incontinent thirst for revenge, and no sooner should they or any of theirs walk abroad in the fields or about the city, but in the shape of a wolf he would presently encounter them, and never rest till he had plucked out their throats and tear their joints asunder. And after he had gotten a taste hereof, he took such pleasure and delight in shedding of blood, that he would night and day walk the fields and work extreme cruelties. And sundry times he would go through the streets of Collin, Bedbur, and Cperadt, in comely habit, and very civilly, as one well known to all the inhabitants thereabout, and oftentimes was he saluted of those whose friends and children he had butchered, though nothing suspected for the same. In these places, I say, he would walk up and down, and if he could spy either maid, wife, or child that his eyes liked or his heart lusted after, he would wait their issuing out of the city or town. If he could by any means get them alone, he would in the fields ravish them, and after in his wolfish likeness cruelly murder them.

Yea, often it came to pass that as he walked abroad in the fields, if he chanced to spy a company of maidens playing together or else a milking their kine, in his wolfish shape he would incontinent run among them, and while the rest escaped by flight, he would be sure to lay hold of one, and after his filthy lust fulfilled, he would murder her presently. Beside, if he had liked or known any of them, look who he had a mind unto, her he would pursue, whether she were before or behind, and take her from the rest, for such was his swiftness of foot while he continued a wolf that he would outrun the swiftest greyhound in that country; and so much he had practiced this wickedness that the whole province was feared by the cruelty of this bloody and devouring wolf.

Thus continuing his devilish and damnable deeds within the compass of a few years, he had murdered thirteen young children, and two goodly young women big with child, tearing the children out of their wombs, in most bloody and savage sort, and after ate their hearts panting hot and raw, which he accounted dainty morsels and best agreeing to his appetite.

Moreover, he used many times to kill lambs and kids and such like beasts, feeding on the same most usually raw and bloody, as if he had been a natural wolf indeed, so that all men mistrusted nothing less than this his devilish sorcery.

He had at that time living a fair young damsel to his daughter, after whom he also lusted must unnaturally, and cruelly committed most wicked incest with her, a most gross and vile sin, far surmounting adultery or fornication, though the least of the three doth drive the soul into hell fire, except hearty repentance,

THE DAMNABLE LIFE AND DEATH

and the great mercy of God. This daughter of his he begot when he was not altogether so wickedly given, who was called by the name of Stubbe Beell, whose beauty and good grace was such as deserved commendations of all those that knew her. And such was his inordinate lust and filthy desire toward her, that he begat a child by her, daily using her as his concubine; but as an insatiate and filthy beast, given over to work evil, with greediness he also lay by his own sister, frequenting her company long time, even according as the wickedness of his heart led him.

Moreover, being on a time sent for to a gossip of his there to make merry and good cheer, ere he thence departed he so won the woman by his fair and flattering speech, and so much prevailed, that ere he departed the house, he lay by her, and ever after had her company at his command. This woman had to name Katherine Trompin, a woman of tall and comely stature of exceeding good favor and one that was well esteemed among her neighbors. But his lewd and inordinate lust being not satisfied with the company of many concubines, nor his wicked fancy contented with the beauty of any woman, at length the Devil sent unto him a wicked spirit in the similitude and likeness of a woman, so fair of face and comely of personage, that she resembled rather some heavenly Helfin than any mortal creature, so far her beauty exceeded the choicest sort of women; and with her, as with his heart's delight, he kept company the space of seven years, though in the end she proved and was found indeed no other than a she-Devil.

Notwithstanding, this lewd sin of lechery did not any thing assuage his cruel and bloody mind, but continuing an insatiable bloodsucker, so great was the joy he took therein, that he accounted no day spent in

OF STUBBE PEETER

pleasure wherein he had not shed some blood, not respecting so much who he did murder, as how to murder and destroy them, as the matter ensuing doth manifest, which may stand for a special note of a cruel and hard heart. For, having a proper youth to his son, begotten in the flower and strength of his age, the first fruit of his body, in whom he took such joy that he did commonly call him his heart's ease, yet so far his delight in murder exceeded the joy he took in his son, that thirsting after his blood, on a time he enticed him into the fields, and from thence into a forest hard by, where, making excuse to stay about the necessaries of nature, while the young man went forward, incontinent in the shape and likeness of a wolf he encountered his own son and there most cruelly slew him, which done, he presently ate the brains out of his head as a most savory and dainty delicious mean to staunch his greedy appetite: the most monstrous act that ever man heard of, for never was known a wretch from nature so far degenerate.

Long time he continued his vile and villainous life, sometime in the likeness of a wolf, sometime in the habit of a man, sometime in the towns and cities, and sometimes in the woods and thickets to them adjoining, whereas the Dutch copy maketh mention, he on a time met with two men and one woman, whom he greatly desired to murder, and the better to bring his devilish purpose to effect, doubting by them to be overmatched and knowing one of them by name, he used this policy to bring them to their end. In subtle sort he conveyed himself far before them in their way and craftily couched out of the sight; but as soon as they approached near the place where he lay, he called one of them by his name. The party, hearing himself called once or twice by his name, supposing it was some familiar friend that in jesting sort stood out of his sight, went from his company toward the place from whence the voice proceeded, of purpose to see who it was; but he was no sooner entered within the danger of this transformed man, but incontinent he was murdered in the place; the rest of his company staying for him, expecting still his return, but finding his stay over long, the other man left the woman and went to look him, by which means the second man was also murdered. The woman then seeing neither of both return again, in heart suspected that some evil had fallen upon them, and therefore, with all the power she had, she sought to save herself by flight, though it nothing prevailed, for, good soul, she was also soon overtaken by this light-footed wolf, whom, when he had first deflowered, he after most cruelly murdered. The men were after found mangled in the wood, but the woman's body was never after seen, for she the caitiff had most ravenously devoured, whose flesh he esteemed both sweet and dainty in taste.

Thus this damnable Stubbe Peeter lived the term of five and twenty years, unsuspected to be author of so many cruel and unnatural murders, in which time he had destroyed and spoiled an unknown number of men, women, and children, sheep, lambs, and goats, and other cattle; for, when he could not through the wariness of people draw men, women, or children in his danger, then, like a cruel and tyrannous beast, he would work his cruelty on brute beasts in most savage sort, and did act more mischief and cruelty than would be credible, although high Germany hath been forced to taste the truth thereof.

By which means the inhabitants of Collin, Bedbur, and Cperadt, seeing themselves so grievously endangered, plagued, and molested by this greedy and

OF STUBBE PEETER

cruel wolf, who wrought continual harm and mischief, insomuch that few or none durst travel to or from those places without good provision of defense, and all for fear of this devouring and fierce wolf, for oftentimes the inhabitants found the arms and legs of dead men, women, and children scattered up and down the fields, to their great grief and vexation of heart, knowing the same to be done by that strange and cruel wolf, whom by no means they could take or overcome, so that if any man or woman missed their child, they were out of hope ever to see it again alive, mistrusting straight that the wolf had destroyed it.

And here is to be noted a most strange thing which setteth forth the great power and merciful providence of God to the comfort of each Christian heart. There were not long ago certain small children playing in a meadow together hard by the town, where also some store of kine were feeding, many of them having young calves sucking upon them. And suddenly among these children comes this vile wolf running and caught a pretty fine girl by the collar, with intent to pull out her throat; but such was the will of God, that the wolf could not pierce the collar of the child's coat, being high and very well stiffened and close clasped about her neck; and therewithal the sudden great cry of the rest of the children which escaped so amazed the cattle feeding by, that being fearful to be robbed of their young, they altogether came running against the wolf with such force that he was presently compelled to let go his hold and to run away to escape the danger of their horns; by which means the child was preserved from death, and, God be thanked, remains living at this day.

An that this thing is true, Master Tice Artine, a brewer dwelling at Puddlewharfe in London, being a

THE DAMNABLE LIFE AND DEATH

man of that country born, and one of good reputation and account, is able to justify, who is near kinsman to this child, and hath from thence twice received letters concerning the same; and for that the first letter did rather drive him into wondering at the act then yielding credit thereunto, he had shortly after, at request of his writing, another letter sent him, whereby he was more fully satisfied; and divers other persons of great credit in London hath in like sort received letters from their friends to the like effect.

Likewise in the town of Germany aforesaid continual prayer was used unto God that it would please Him to deliver them from the danger of this greedy wolf.

And, although they had practiced all the means that men could devise to take this ravenous beast, yet until the Lord had determined his fall, they could not in any wise prevail: notwithstanding, they daily continued their purpose, and daily sought to entrap him, and for that intent continually maintained great mastiffs and dogs of much strength to hunt and chase the beast. In the end, it pleased God, as they were in readiness and provided to meet with him, that they should espy him in his wolfish likeness at what time they beset him round about, and most circumspectly set their dogs upon him, in such sort that there was no means of escape, at which advantage they never could get him before; but as the Lord delivered Goliath into the hands of David, so was this wolf brought in danger of these men, who seeing, as I said before, no way to escape the imminent danger, being hardly pursued at the heels, presently slipped his girdle from about him, whereby the shape of a wolf clean avoided, and he appeared presently in his true shape and likeness, having in his hand a staff as one walking toward the city. But the hunters, whose eyes were steadfastly bent upon the beast, and seeing him in the same place metamorphosed contrary to their expectation, it wrought a wonderful amazement to their minds; and, had it not been that they knew the man so soon as they saw him, they had surely taken the same to have been some Devil in a man's likeness; but for as much as they knew him to be an ancient dweller in the town, they came unto him, and talking with him, they brought him by communication home to his own house, and finding him to be the man indeed, and no delusion or fantastical motion, they had him incontinent before the magistrates to be examined.

Thus being apprehended, he was shortly after put to the rack in the town of Bedbur, but fearing the torture, he voluntarily confessed his whole life, and made known the villainies which he had committed for the space of 25 years; also he confessed how by sorcery he procured of the Devil a girdle, which being put on, he forthwith became a wolf, which girdle at his apprehension he confessed he cast it off in a certain valley and there left it, which, when the magistrates heard, they sent to the valley for it, but at their coming found nothing at all, for it may be supposed that it was gone to the Devil from whence it came, so that it was not to be found. For the Devil having brought the wretch to all the shame he could, left him to endure the torments which his deeds deserved.

After he had some space been imprisoned, the magistrates found out through due examination of the matter, that his daughter Stubbe Beell and his gossip Katherine Trompin were both accessory to divers murders committed, who for the same as also for their lewd life otherwise committed, was arraigned, and with Stubbe Peeter condemned, and their several

THE DAMNABLE LIFE AND DEATH

judgments pronounced the 28 of October 1589, in this manner, that is to say: Stubbe Peeter as principal malefactor, was judged first to have his body laid on a wheel, and with red hot burning pincers in ten several places to have the flesh pulled off from the bones, after that, his legs and arms to be broken with a wooden ax or hatchet, afterward to have his head struck from his body, then to have his carcass burned to ashes.

Also his daughter and his gossip were judged to be burned quick to ashes, the same time and day with the carcass of the aforesaid Stubbe Peeter. And on the 31st of the same month, they suffered death accordingly in the town of Bedbur in the presence of many peers and princes of Germany.

This, Gentle Reader, have I set down the true discourse of this wicked man Stub Peeter, which I desire to be a warning to all sorcerers and witches, which unlawfully follow their own devilish imagination to the utter ruin and destruction of their souls eternally, from which wicked and damnable practice, I beseech God keep all good men, and from the cruelty of their wicked hearts. Amen.

After the execution, there was by the advice of the magistrates of the town of Bedbur a high pole set up and strongly framed, which first went through the wheel whereon he was broken, whereunto also it was fastened; after that a little above the wheel the likeness of a wolf was framed in wood, to show unto all men the shape wherein he executed those cruelties. Over that on the top of the stake the sorcerer's head itself was set up, and round about the wheel there hung as it were sixteen pieces of wood about a yard in length with represented the sixteen persons that was perfectly known to be murdered by him. And the same

OF STUBBE PEETER

ordained to stand there for a continual monument to all ensuing ages, what murders by Stub Peeter was committed, with the order of his judgment, as this picture doth more plainly express.

Witnesses that this is true: Tyse Artyne. William Brewar. Adolf Staedt. George Bores. With divers others that have seen the same.

OTHER BOOKS ABOUT THE SUPERNATURAL FROM CURIOUS PUBLICATIONS

The History of Spiritualism (Vols. 1 & 2)
by Sir Arthur Conan Doyle

The Case for Spirit Photography
by Sir Arthur Conan Doyle

True Ghost Stories
by Hereward Carrington

*Spectropia, or Surprising Spectral Illusions
Showing Ghosts Everywhere*
by J. H. Brown

Spirit Slate Writing and Kindred Phenomena
by William E. Robinson

How to Speak With the Dead: A Practical Handbook
by Sciens

*The Talking Dead: A Collection of Messages from
Beyond the Veil, 1850s-1920s*
Edited by Marc Hartzman

Vampires and Vampirism
by Dudley Wright

The Book of Dreams and Ghosts
by Andrew Lang

curiouspublications.com

www.ingramcontent.com/pod-product-compliance
Lightning Source LLC
Chambersburg PA
CBHW020443030426
42337CB00014B/1371